Case Study

Village Animal Healthcare

A community-based approach to livestock
development in Kenya

Barbara Grandin, Ramesh Thampy, John Young

ITDG
PUBLISHING

Published by ITDG Publishing
The Schumacher Centre for Technology and Development
Bourton Hall, Bourton-on-Dunsmore, Rugby, Warwickshire CV23 9QZ, UK
www.itdgpublishing.org.uk

First published in 1991
Reprinted 1994
Print on demand since 2004

ISBN 1 85339 092 5

A catalogue record for this book is available
from the British Library

ITDG Publishing is the publishing arm of the Intermediate Technology
Development Group. Our mission is to build the skills and capacity of people
in developing countries through the dissemination of information in all forms,
enabling them to improve the quality of their lives and that of future generations.

Printed in Great Britain by Lightning Source, Milton Keynes

Barbara Grandin is a Social Anthropologist, with considerable experience of livestock work in Africa. She worked at the ILCA (International Livestock Centre for Africa), and most recently, as social anthropologist on Vet Epidemiology and Socio-economic Unit of ILRAD (International Laboratory for Research on animal diseases).

Ramesh Thampy is a vet, who has worked as a Veterinary Officer in the Rift Valley Province of Kenya, with Action Aid and as a Livestock Project Advisor for CARE Kenya. He is currently working with the World Wildlife Fund working on integrated environment and land use project around Lake Nakuru, Kenya.

John Young worked with Voluntary Service Overseas as veterinarian to a milk producers' association in Sri Lanka, and in farm animal practice in the UK, before going to Kenya on behalf of ITDG in 1986. Since late 1989 he has been based in the UK as manager for Intermediate Technology's Livestock programme.

CONTENTS

INTRODUCTION 1

Background to the programme 1
The setting 3

THE PROJECTS 9

Kamujini Farmers' Centre (KFC), Meru District 9
Kenya Freedom From Hunger Council (KFFHC),
Baringo District 18
Utooni Development Project (UDP),
Machakos District 24
Oxfam, Samburu District 28

DISCUSSION AND CONCLUSIONS 30

The technical content of the programme 30
KLP's relationships with project partners 36
Sustainability 37
Outlook for the future 40

NOTES 41

APPENDICES 43

Appendix 1:   The objectives of the Agriculture and
               Fisheries Sector and of the Kenya
               Livestock Programme 43
Appendix 2:   Social, cultural and livestock data
               for the project sites 44
Appendix 3:   Disease incidence and the provision
               of veterinary services in the
               project areas 49

ABBREVIATIONS AND ACRONYMS

AEZ	Agro-ecological zone
AHA	Animal Health Assistant
APO	Animal Production Officer
ASAL	Arid and Semi-arid lands
ATB	Agricultural Training Board (UK)
CAFAW	Community Animal First Aid Worker
CAFOD	Catholic Fund for Overseas Development
CBPP	Contagious bovine pleuropneumonia
CCPP	Contagious caprine Pleuropneumonia
CIIR	Catholic Institute for International Relations
DAH	Decentralized Animal Health
DAHS	Decentralized Animal Health Service
DANIDA	Danish Government Aid Organization
DDC	District Development Committee
DVO	District Veterinary Officer
DVS	District Veterinary Services
ECF	East Coast fever
EPAP	East Pokot Agricultural Project
FMD	Foot and Mouth Disease
FMH	Farm Management Handbook
GAA	German Agro-Action
GoK	Government of Kenya
ITDG	Intermediate Technology Development Group
ITK	Indigenous Technical Knowledge
JAHR	Junior Animal Health Assistant
KFC	Kamujini Farmers Centre
KFFHC	Kenya Freedom from Hunger Council
KLP	Kenya Livestock Programme
KVA	Kenya Veterinary Association
LO	Livestock Officer
MLD	Ministry of Livestock Development
NCCSS	National Council of Culture and Social Services
NGO	Non-Government Organization
NORAD	Norwegian Overseas Aid Organization
RVP	Rift Valley Province
TLU	Tropical Livestock Unit
VO	Veterinary Officer
WR	Wealth Rank

KENYAN WORDS USED IN THE TEXT

Borana	Tribal name
Dawa	Medicine
Duka ya dawa	Shop selling medicine
Msaidizi	'Helper' – abbreviated form of Msaidizi wa Mifugo: 'Helper of Livestock'
Musyi	Extended family
Njoka	Worms
Wananchi	The people – citizens
Wasaidizi	Plural form of Msaidizi

INTRODUCTION

Background to the programme

The Kenya Livestock Programme began in 1986 when ITDG was invited to assist with the establishment of a series of training courses for farmers and community animal health workers ('barefoot vets') at Kamujini Farmers' Centre in Meru District, central Kenya. Staff at the Centre had heard about the programme's previous work in Gujarat in India, involving 'barefoot vets' who traditionally treated animals in their localities. Coverage of remote rural areas by the existing veterinary service was poor, and the programme had sent a vet to assist staff of the Vivekanand Research and Training Institute to train barefoot vets and farmers from local villages. The training provided basic information on the diagnosis and treatment of simple diseases, including some traditional herbal remedies, and on preventive measures. A primary animal first aid kit was supplied to trainees, plus medicines for them to use and sell.

ITDG is an independent organization which aims to improve the situation of poor rural producers in the developing world through the introduction of appropriate technologies. The Kenya Livestock Programme (KLP) is part of its Agriculture and Fisheries Sector. The sector's mandate can be found in Appendix 1. KLP aims to help resource-poor households find ways to maintain or increase livestock production, or the efficiency of utilization of their products, and to improve food production and income. Appendix 1 also includes an outline of the programme's long- and medium-term objectives.

KLP aims to target the poorest people in a project area and build on their existing expertise. The programme's approach thus needs to be 'socially sensitive' and, before beginning any technical activity, emphasis is placed on data collection to determine who are the poorest and how best they can be assisted. Attempts are also made to identify the extent of existing knowledge and activity, which will provide a starting point for technical training, and to obtain baseline data against which

1

projects can be monitored. Rather than setting up its own 'operational' projects, ITDG works through local organizations – its 'project partners'. These are usually indigenous non-government organizations (NGOs), but may also be local representatives of international NGOs or national governments. A related aim of the programme is the achievement of 'sustainability' – the ability of local people (and their organizations) to continue, and build on, project activity when external inputs have ceased. Thus, as well as providing technical inputs, KLP's objectives include improving other aspects of their partners' capacity to undertake project activities, such as financial and management training. In addition to this 'capacity building', sustainability depends on favourable government policy, which the programme also seeks to influence.

During the early information collection phase of the work with Kamujini Farmers' Centre it was realized that animal health was a serious problem for the region's poor farmers , who were not being reached by existing veterinary services, and it was therefore thought that some form of decentralized animal health (DAH) programme might be useful. At that time the concept of 'barefoot vets' was relatively new in east Africa. However, from its beginning at Kamujini in 1986 the programme has been involved in over a dozen different projects in Kenya in which one form of DAH has been tested in different agro-ecological and social situations.

In August 1989 it was decided that KLP's first three years of operation should be reviewed. The primary function of the review was to provide guidance to ITDG for the development of the programme over the next few years by assessing the effectiveness of its activities to date in social, economic and technical terms, including both the content of the programme and the way KLP had worked with its collaborating organizations.

This publication contains the main findings of the review. The remainder of this section outlines the setting for the projects in terms of Kenya's agro-ecology, livestock production and disease incidence and the existing veterinary service. In the next section the four main projects undertaken by KLP are described, including recommendations for

2

future work. The third section provides a summary of the main discussions and conclusions of the review, highlighting aspects of the programme's methodology, and an outline of KLP's plans for the future.

The setting

Kenya, ranging from Lake Victoria and the Ugandan escarpment in the west to the Indian ocean in the east, with Mount Kenya in the middle, covers a wide range of ecological environments dictated largely by altitude and rainfall. These environments include regions of intensive agricultural production (zones 1 to 3), marginal agriculture and livestock (zones 4 and 5) and nomadic pastoralism (zones 6 and 7). The distribution of these zones is shown in Figure 1. Kenya's population is similarly varied, having an enormous number of distinct ethnic groups each with their own language, culture and social organization.

Agriculture continues to dominate Kenya's economy, although its share of Gross Domestic Product (GDP) has declined slightly in recent years. Production grew by an average of 2.5 per cent each year between 1983 and 1988.[1] Eighty per cent of the country's working population make their living on the land, while 22 per cent of the people in paid employment are in the agricultural sector. More than 50 per cent of the country's total agricultural output is subsistence production.

The production of meat and milk accounts for a significant proportion of Kenya's total agricultural production. Livestock production is an important economic activity for large numbers of rural people, and the only economic activity for the 25 per cent of the population who live in arid areas. There are approximately 11 million cattle, 6 million sheep, 8 million goats, 0.5 million camels and 150,000 donkeys in Kenya.[2] More than half of these livestock are to be found in the semi-arid areas of the country. In 1988 annual demand for milk within Kenya outstripped production by 526,000 tonnes and demand for beef outstripped production by 110,000 tonnes.[3] A major contribution to this poor performance is the widespread occurrence of preventable livestock diseases.

3

Figure 1
Map of Kenya showing the major agro-ecological zones

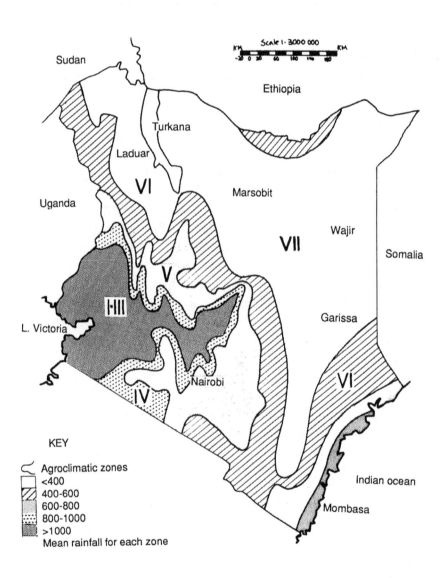

Livestock disease incidence [4]

Helminthiasis (worms and flukes), foot and mouth disease (FMD), tick-borne diseases such as *anaplasmosis* and *east coast fever* (ECF), and *trypanosomiasis* are the major diseases affecting the large ruminants, *trypanosomiasis* and FMD being endemic in most districts. *Rinderpest* occurs sporadically, as do *contagious bovine pleuropneumonia* (CBPP), anthrax, black quarter and lumpy skin disease. Other common bovine diseases include *mastitis, enteritis,* eye infections, retained afterbirths and pneumonias. *Helminthiasis* and foot rot together account for more than a third of the diseases reported for sheep and goats. *Contagious caprine pleuropneumonia* (CCPP) is enzootic in many districts and is reported to be the single most limiting factor to goat production.

Prevention of diseases such as *anaplasmosis* and ECF is dependent on efficient tick control, and successful treatment hinges on early diagnosis and treatment. These diseases have high morbidity and mortality rates and a prolonged recovery period. Infestations of *helminths* exert a negative effect on productivity long before the appearance of clinical signs, and farmers often suffer losses of production without being aware of an infection. Heavy infestations can cause mortalities. Major constraints to the control of these diseases are a lack of knowledge on the part of farmers of their symptoms and infectivity, in addition to a limited availability of drugs.

Vaccination campaigns are carried out by veterinary staff against a number of diseases, the FMD campaign being the most extensive in terms of geographical coverage. Vaccinations against sporadically occurring diseases are usually undertaken only in response to a fresh outbreak. However, full coverage of all susceptible animals is rarely achieved in the campaigns, due to operational difficulties and, in cases such as CCPP, non-availability of vaccine. Thus serious diseases are perpetuated and are likely to remain a problem in the foreseeable future.

In the absence of reliable data (both epidemiological and economic) it is impossible to quantify precisely the economic losses incurred as a result of livestock diseases in Kenya. A conservative

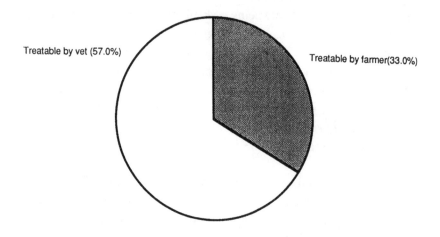

Figure 2
Bovine diseases treatable by farmer and vet
(for total cases seen in RVP in 1987)

Treatable by vet (57.0%)

Treatable by farmer(33.0%)

Figure 3
Bovine diseases treatable by trained farmers
(approximately 33% of cases treated)

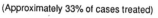

(Approximately 33% of cases treated)

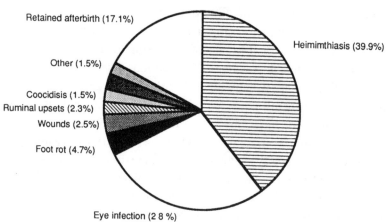

Retained afterbirth (17.1%)

Heimimthiasis (39.9%)

Other (1.5%)

Coocidisis (1.5%)
Ruminal upsets (2.3%)
Wounds (2.5%)

Foot rot (4.7%)

Eye infection (2 8 %)

estimate places the loss at about US$43 million per annum but, as the economic loss due to *helminth* infestations in sheep alone has been estimated at approximately US$26 million per annum,[5] this is probably an underestimate. It is possible that equally high losses are incurred as a result of *helminthiasis* in cattle and goats, as most sheep helminths are even more infective to goats than sheep.[6] It is estimated that about 70,000 cattle die of ECF annually in Kenya,[7] which alone would account for a loss of US$6 million. The losses incurred as a result of sporadically occurring diseases such as rinderpest and CCPP have not been evaluated.

Kenya's veterinary service

In Kenya as elsewhere veterinary services operate both at the national or state level, to deal with potential or real disease outbreaks affecting large numbers of animals, and at the level of the individual farmer. From the point of view of the Kenyan livestock owner, the latter is of greater importance because of its immediate help in avoiding or reducing financial loss. In contrast to the developed world, the private practitioner service in Kenya is very rudimentary and the responsibility for providing veterinary services at both national and farm levels has fallen to the Department of Veterinary Services (DVS). However, the department is constrained by a lack of funds and transport facilities and an inconsistent supply of drugs. Staffing levels are also low, varying from a ratio of 1:1,000 TLU[8] in high-potential areas to 1:13,000 TLU in the pastoral districts. Thus, in general, the veterinary service is inadequate to meet the needs of the livestock sector.

In addition to the scarcity of veterinary staff in pastoral districts, the vastness of the area, the scattering of people and their herds, and the poor roads and communications all hinder the efficient supervision of farmers and the monitoring and treatment of livestock diseases. The higher livestock population in these areas and the characteristics of the pastoral production system, including frequent nutritional gaps and the concentration of animals around water holes, facilitate the acquisition and spread of diseases. Thus there is a particular need for auxiliary animal health services in the pastoral districts of the country.

Many of the common animal diseases are amenable to diagnosis and treatment by trained farmers, without recourse to scheduled drugs. Figure 2 shows the proportion of total bovine diseases which could be treated by farmers, and Figure 3 the relative importance of each disease. The proportions for goats and sheep are similar; thus training farmers in only a few common diseases would greatly relieve the workload of government veterinary staff, leaving them more time to deal with serious cases.

THE PROJECTS

Kamujini Farmers' Centre (KFC), Meru District

KFC was the first ITDG livestock project in Kenya and, as mentioned in the introduction, KLP was asked in 1986 to help train farmers and barefoot vets (*wasaidizi*, or *msaidizi* in the singular) as part of the centre's livestock development programme. KFC is run by the Catholic Diocese of Meru as an agricultural training and extension centre and its other activities include income-generating projects for women's groups, agricultural extension through farmers' groups, and building water tanks.

The project area covers 350km^2, with a population of about 45,000 people and 9,000 households according to the 1979 census. (The 1990 levels are likely to be 25-50 per cent higher). Land scarcity is a serious and ever-increasing problem and is leading to the intensification of many agricultural activities, including livestock-rearing. Demarcation of government Tribal Trust Land into farms with individual freehold title has been under way for almost twenty years, but only a small portion of the land has been registered.

As can be seen from Figures 1 and 4, Meru generally falls in the medium-potential agro-ecological zones (4 and 5). However, the project covers portions of two divisions (Tigania and Tharaka) which differ in their detailed agro-ecology and ethnic subgroups. The Meruians who live in the higher potential area were traditionally agriculturalists, although livestock-keeping, especially of cattle, has always been an important economic and social activity. Among these Meruians, Tiganians appear to have more cattle than other subgroups. The Tharakan area is of much lower agro-ecological potential. Tharakans traditionally practised shifting cultivation, combined with hunting, bee-keeping and livestock rearing, with rather more emphasis on goats than cattle. Nevertheless, cattle are an important source both of livelihood and, increasingly, of traction, and are kept by 85 per cent of Tharakan households.

9

Figure 4
Map of Kenya showing major project sites

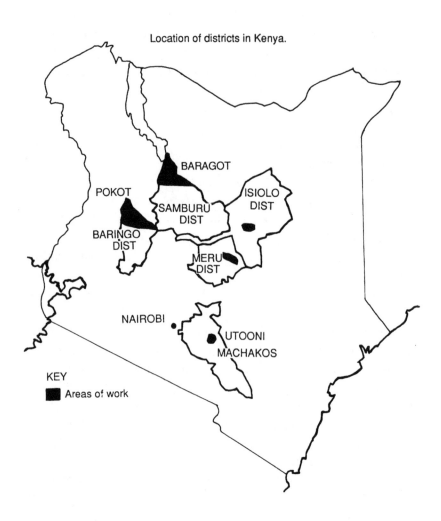

Location of districts in Kenya.

Some of the basic information on agriculture and livestock holdings in the Meru project sites can be found in Tables 1 & 2, Appendix 2.[9] It is quite clear that there are important agro-ecological differences between the sites, and equally important differences across wealth rank. The Tigania area is much better watered and has more lucrative cash crops, and the keeping of grade cattle under semi-intensive management occurs among wealthier households. As would be expected, more rich households own animals (especially cattle) and own far more of them. As KLP was anxious that resource-poor farmers should not be excluded from project benefits, a special effort was made to focus efforts on smallstock and chickens which are more important to poorer households. A conscious decision was made to not pursue research and extension on the management needs of improved cattle (a type of programme common in higher potential areas of the country), which would benefit only the rich farmers in the area.

Data collection

As Meru was the first project site, a generous amount of time was devoted to baseline data collection. This included several months of informal data collection and literature review, although unfortunately there is little material available on contemporary Meru agriculture or social organization. Initial investigations were followed by a fairly detailed one-shot survey, covering 129 farmers from 10 villages. The villages were selected by a stratified sampling design to represent the area in terms of agro-ecological zone, wealth, proximity to markets and time of settlement. Farmers representative of rich, average and poor households in each village were chosen using a rapid rural appraisal technique known as wealth ranking.[10]

The questionnaire used in the survey covered cultivation and land holding, sources of cash income in normal and drought years, and livestock numbers, functions and problems by species. Last incidence of disease and death by species and age category were also elicited. This was coupled with formal data collection from other farmers on ethno-veterinary knowledge and the disposition of progeny of animals born on

11

the farm. At several points in the questionnaire farmers were asked to identify problems they had, for example with feeding, breeding and animal health, and possible ways in which KFC might help. Sources of veterinary treatment were also recorded.

The survey found a disease-related mortality rate of 22 per cent for cattle and 18 per cent for goats. Sixty-four per cent of cattle owners reported a cow sick in the last year, and 17 per cent reported the death of a cow or calf in the period. Fifty-five per cent of goat and sheep owners reported an animal sick, and 43 per cent a death. The most common disease affecting all livestock was worms, followed by *anaplasmosis* and ECF in cattle and pneumonia in goats and sheep. (For further details on disease incidence in Tigania Division, see Tables 1 and 2 in Appendix 3). Table 3 in Appendix 3 shows the number of DVS personnel in Meru in relation to the sizes of the two divisions and their livestock and human populations. The provision of veterinary services is generally poor and appears to be biased in favour of the higher potential area, and only the veterinary officer in Tigania has access to transport.

For ruminants, feeding was the most common problem cited by farmers, with disease and drug shortages coming second and third. For chickens, disease was the most commonly cited problem, followed by feed supply. As suggested above, lack of veterinary inputs was felt to be particularly severe in the lower, drier areas. When farmers were asked what help KFC might provide, the most common response was a veterinary drug store, followed by a veterinarian on the staff. Farmers in the Tharaka area were virtually unanimous in listing improved drug supplies, presumably reflecting both the more important role of livestock in their agro-pastoral economy and the relative lack of drug availability there as compared to Tigania, which is closer to market centres. Management advice and improved water supplies were also mentioned.

The informal and formal surveys indicated the existence of traditional livestock disease specialists (*mugaa*) whom people still occasionally consult. Self-treatment with both traditional and western

12

drugs was commonly reported for local cattle, smallstock and chickens; occasionally neighbours were called. Government veterinary services were used largely by the rich, especially the wealthy owners of European breed or crossbreed cattle. However, the studies led to the conclusion that, in general, the level of indigenous technical knowledge was not great. Ordinary farmers were able to name only a few diseases, symptom recognition seemed crude, and many farmers said they had never felt the need to call a vet because they never had a sick animal. In addition the use of anti-helminthics was low, especially with indigenous stock.

Compared to agricultural information, relatively less emphasis was placed on collecting information about social organization in Meru. Key informants were used to outline certain social organizational factors, including definition of the household, the community and possible sub-divisions within the community, but their role and functions were not described in depth. Villages were traditionally clan-based, although migration has now led to mixtures of clans within villages. However, clan membership is still an important source of identity, providing the primary social security network of individuals. Other ties between individuals involve factors such as marriage and neighbourhood. A variety of organized groups exist in the area (farmers', women's, youth, etc.), many having been started by KFC. The women's groups are the most active, largely due to the continued presence and efforts of VSO (Voluntary Service Overseas) volunteers at KFC.

The same 129 farmers involved in the initial survey were interviewed again in August – September 1988, as part of a household level monitoring exercise (to complement the *wasaidizi's* own records of farmers seen and animals treated). They were asked what, if anything, they knew of the *wasaidizi* service, if they had used it and their evaluation of it, as well as ways in which extension messages could better reach people. Another aim of the second survey was the establishment of further monitoring procedures.

13

Training of wasaidizi

Based on the relatively low level of indigenous technical knowledge found in the Meru project areas, it was decided to focus exclusively on the training of intermediaries. The way in which the training was organized was determined to a large extent by the structure of KFC; the centre's extension had traditionally been carried out with groups, so community contact was made through a variety of those with existing affiliations. The groups were asked to select someone to be trained for their village, it being made clear that this person would be expected to serve more than just group members.

Thirteen *wasaidizi* were trained in August 1987 and a further 14 in August 1988. In addition, 24 women from various women's groups were trained to vaccinate chickens against Newcastle disease (a major problem in the area). As this was the first KLP project, at the time people were chosen to train as *wasaidizi* the likely workload and profit were all unknown. Thus, although some selection criteria were proposed by the project, they could not be sufficiently detailed and inevitably some less-than-ideal candidates were chosen. However, by the time of the second round of training, better selection seems to have occurred as both groups and potential candidates had a clearer understanding of the role of *wasaidizi*.

The training included discussion about the common diseases and, building on the *wasaidizi*'s existing knowledge of traditional herbal remedies, the use of simple medicines to treat conditions such as worms, wounds, mange and ticks. After training, the *wasaidizi* were given a kit of medicines and equipment. They then returned to their villages to provide a simple animal health service for their neighbours, for which they would make a charge to include the cost of the medicines and a small profit. When medicines were finished they could use their profits to buy more.

In the 17-month period from September 1987 to January 1989 the *wasaidizi* treated 2,679 cattle, 1,771 smallstock, 85 chickens, 101 dogs, 11 donkeys and 2 rabbits; a total of over 4,600 animals. (This compares to estimated project populations of 35,000 cattle, 86,000 smallstock,

14

As part of wsaidizi *training, paticipants are taught how to make a halter for livestock.*

15

and 126,000 chickens.) This gives an average of about 17 animals per *msaidizi* per month; a figure which would be considerably higher if it excluded those early *wasaidizi* who were poorly selected, several of whom treated very few animals and have more or less dropped out of the project. Of the treatments 2,365 (or about 50 per cent) were for worms, and over 6,000 chickens were vaccinated for Newcastle disease in the course of the project.

In addition to treating animals the *wasaidizi* sold some drugs to farmers whom they could not visit, direct sales accounting for about 20 per cent of farmer contacts. Another important component of the Meru project was the establishment of a shop (duka ya dawa) to supply the simple drugs (dawas) used by *wasaidizi*. The shop was originally situated at KFC, but this was inconvenient for many areas and a new shop was opened in the major highland market town in 1988.

User perceptions and recommendations for future activity
Indications from the second survey were that farmers in the Meru area were pleased with the *wasaidizi* service, and even the simple drugs provided had been well accepted by the community. There were numerous requests for the training of more *wasaidizi* to ensure greater coverage. (A few *wasaidizi* fear this as they are afraid it will cut into their profits). The primary complaint about the *wasaidizi* was that they do not carry serious drugs which, given current legislation, they are prohibited from doing. The extension efforts should reinforce to farmers (and even to *wasaidizi*, not all of whom appear conversant with government restrictions) the legal status of serious drugs. Attempts have been made to improve liaison with the government veterinary department for cases which need referral.

The *wasaidizi* themselves felt that the most useful part of their training had been learning about disease recognition – two who were assessed as part of the review said the course had covered diseases with which they were previously completely unfamiliar. They also mentioned the value of learning about effective dosages, and indicated that

16

traditional remedies were being abandoned in favour of more 'progressive' dawas.

Based on information elicited from the two surveys, it can be stated that farmers who know about the programme have, on the whole, not hesitated to use it if they have felt a need. Their low level of knowledge of animal disease prevention and treatment is a more serious hindrance to the use of the service. In keeping with the findings of the initial survey, the main reason cited by farmers in the second survey for never having asked a *msaidizi* to visit was that animals were rarely sick. Alternatively farmers were only requesting treatment in the late stages of illness, after much productivity had been lost and when treatment was more difficult. Thus, although the decision to train intermediaries was the most appropriate for the circumstances, as the project matures *wasaidizi* should be encouraged to explain to clients the symptoms they see, their diagnosis and treatment, and farmers should receive some direct training on the most common simple diseases and symptom recognition.

The variety of ties between individuals in Meru District, as identified in the initial survey, has undoubtedly helped to ensure that the *wasaidizi* serve a broad base of people in their villages, although follow-up surveys have suggested that some biases do exist. One important source of bias stems from the fact that KFC started work in Tigania, and virtually all the staff are Tiganians who feel some measure of discomfort in dealing with Tharakans. In addition the overwhelming proportion of *wasaidizi* trained, and the first drug shops opened, were in Tigania. However, a new Tharakan extension worker has recently been hired who should begin to redress some of the bias in project activity towards Tigania.

The method of selecting people from existing groups to train as *wasaidizi* does not appear to have created any difficulties, with the exception that sometimes a group member or a relative of an influential group member would be chosen when they might not be the most suitable type of person. Insufficient information is available to determine to what extent there might be socio-economic biases in group membership which affect the outreach of the project. The follow-up survey clearly showed that many people in the project area, even some close to KFC, were unaware of the *wasaidizi*. There is some evidence from wealth ranking that group membership is dominated by wealthier households and that groups do not represent the village as a whole, but rather some, as yet unknown, sub-segment.

With clans no longer providing a basis for local communities, there is no traditional village-level council of elders or other group to serve as community-level organ of access. Hence the model used was the only one possible, but further extension should seek to work through a wider range of groups. In addition, with the exception of the chicken work, the poorest people in the higher areas probably do not benefit from the *wasaidizi* service as they have almost no livestock. Poorer households in the low, drier areas do keep livestock, but further information is required to determine the extent to which they have used *wasaidizi* and how the service could more closely meet their needs.

The shop was an important step forward in increasing farmers' access to veterinary supplies, and the small monthly profit was evpected to cover running costs within twoyears. It was planned that the attendant (herself trained as an *msaidizi*) would assume responsibility for reprovisioning (supplies are purchased at wholesale rates from a chemist in Meru) and a second shop was planned for the dry areas.

The project itself has just been extended for a second three-year period, during which time the barefoot vet training will be consolidated and expanded. In addition, KLP will begin to train farmers in simple improvements to existing management systems which will increase the productivity of their livestock.

Kenya Freedom From Hunger Council (KFFHC), Baringo District

In Pokot, Baringo District, ITDG was asked by KFFHC and the East Pokot Agricultural Project (EPAP) to implement the animal health

18

component of their joint livestock development project by training community animal first aid workers (CAFAWs). KLP began work in Pokot in July 1987.

In contrast to Meru, Baringo is a semi-arid area, falling in agro-ecological zones 6 and 7 (see Figures 1 and 4). The project is based in Nginyang Division and involves five widely spaced communities. The East Pokot are a short-range, transhumant pastoral people; they have 'home areas' where the bulk of the household and smallstock stay throughout normal years, while young men and cattle move to highland locations in search of dry season grazing. Although there are no cultural constraints to changing one's home area (and producers do so), there are distinct advantages in remaining in the same home area in terms of social ties and knowledge of local conditions.

The project sites vary in agro-ecological conditions (based to a large extent on altitude, and hence moisture availability, and the possibility of cropping) and the socio-economic status of the people who live there. For example at one site, Chesanja, very near the mission, cropping is not feasible and the inhabitants are relatively poorer households who depend on casual labour to supplement their pastoral livelihoods. Another site, Kechii, is inhabited by a group of Pokot who are on the whole far wealthier. Although Chepelion is high, cropping is an important activity but it is too cold for camel-keeping.

Relatively more is known about the social organization of the Pokot than of the agricultural project communities. Households usually consist of a man, his wives and two or three children, with the occasional incorporation of a married son and children or other dependents. Occasionally households join together for residence and herding. These seem to be temporary arrangements and there is no Pokot word for this 'compound' unit. Households are grouped into larger units – *'mangot'* – which might be called neighbourhoods or villages. The neighbourhood is the unit which controls local grazing and watering resources, control being exercised through a council of household heads called the *'kokwa'* which served as the point of contact for the project.

19

Data collection

In Pokot, data collection possibilities were highly constrained by the lack of time and other resources, and the level of background information available through the project was poor. Wealth ranking was used as a primary data-gathering technique rather than as a tool for sample stratification. Households were ranked as usual, but this was followed by detailed discussions to elicit information on access to resources (in this system, essentially livestock). Progeny histories and ethno-veterinary data collection were also undertaken to provide estimates of livestock fertility, mortality and animal offtake, and to assess the level of indigenous technical knowledge.[11]

Although systematic sampling of the population in the area was not undertaken, combining data from the five sites provided a rough idea of livestock holdings (Table 3, Appendix 2). This information was derived by asking farmers to estimate the number of livestock of each species which would be owned by producers in each wealth rank. As KLP has found in many sites, there is significant variation in livestock ownership by both area and wealth rank in Pokot, goats being more important to poor people than cattle. It was thus decided that training courses would concentrate on goats.

Although no formal question about livestock-related needs was put to the communities, it became clear at the end of the first round of data collection that disease was a major cause of livestock loss. Questions to farmers identified disease as causing the loss of between 44 per cent and 62 per cent of livestock, with the commonest diseases causing the death of cattle being east coast fever and trypanosomiasis. Diarrhoea, worms and pneumonia were the main causes of death in goats and sheep. Veterinary staff at the time, however, identified internal and external parasites as the most important livestock disease problems, although they tend to cause loss of production rather than death. Data on causes of death among livestock in Nginyang Division, Baringo District are presented in Table 3, Appendix 3.

The number of DVS staff in Nginyang Division, together with the human and livestock populations, can be seen in Table 3 of Appendix

3. If the area was divided equitably between the 13 veterinary personnel, each would have to cover an area of 342km², serve 324 households and be responsible for the health of 3,780 TLUs. As only one of the officers has access to transport, this is an impossible task. In addition to the lack of transport and frequent shortages of drugs, veterinary personnel in Nginyang are actively involved in the vaccination campaigns for between three and six months of the year. This drastically reduces the time available for the provision of routine clinical services, and animal health extension services in the area are almost non-existent.

In contrast to Meru, initial investigations found that the Pokot had a considerable traditional and modern knowledge of livestock diseases. However, lack of veterinary drugs, and knowledge about proper dose rates were flagged as important problems. As with every other project, the issue of gazetted drugs was recognized to be critical and project extension staff were given government permission to keep a limited range of serious drugs.

In the course of the project further qualitative information was collected in order to monitor the CAFAWs, obtain community feedback and assess the viability of the project design.

Training of CAFAWs
The first two training courses (for KFFHC extension workers and then CAFAWs) were held in October 1987. On the basis of the limited information available, and given the success of the model used for the Meru project, the Pokot project was designed along similar lines. Thus every *kokwa* in each of the project areas was asked to nominate two people to be trained. The course was similar to that in Meru, with modifications mainly due to the different level of pre-existing knowledge and the need to train extension workers in the use of more serious drugs. However, unlike Meru where the shop was opened to sell medicines to the *wasaidizi*, medicines for the CAFAWs were purchased by the project in Pokot and then sold to them by the project extension workers.

In their first 12 months of operation, the ten CAFAWs trained paid over 1,500 visits to farmers and treated almost 7,000 animals. Of these, 3 per cent were camels, 12 per cent cattle and 85 per cent goats. (This compares to an estimated distribution of animals as 1 per cent camels, 29 per cent cattle and 70 per cent goats). Of the treatments, 53 per cent were for ticks and 36 per cent for worms. The amount of tick treatment grew significantly after February 1988 when several of the CAFAWs were issued with spray pumps (to replace the hand washing of animals). However, it is not clear whether the pumps continued to function as they are not repairable in the area. In terms of the impact of the programme, however, even if spraying by CAFAWs is removed from consideration, the number of animals treated is still large and the proportions by species are almost the same.[12]

User perceptions and recommendations for future activity

The KFFHC project had evolved from famine relief to food for work to development. The project sites were chosen in part because of the success of earlier efforts in those areas. Exactly what sort of biases this has led to remains uncertain. The reports of ITDG staff have indicated that, overall, there does not seem to be any pattern of bias by CAFAWs against non-project members or poor households. Although in some areas (such as Chepelion) relatively few poor households are served, this is hardly surprising when the poorest third (of the project members in that area) have only four livestock units per household. Generally, however, data indicate that producers of all wealth ranks, and both project and non-project members, are being served. As noted above, proportionately more camels and goats were treated by the CAFAWs and proportionately fewer cattle. Reasons for this might be explored as part ofcontinuing work in the area.

The village council of elders was the logical point of access to each community as it represents the decision-making group for the area's community affairs. At any given meeting, however, unless it is for a major event, only a few members are present. It would be useful for several of the areas to determine whether there is a wealth bias in *kokwa*

22

attendance. If there is, care must be taken in using only *kokwa*-based feedback. A second problem which emerges in using the *kokwa* as the sole point of access is that 'members' are all men. To the extent that women have responsibilities for certain aspects of livestock management (for instance, the care of young stock), it might be useful for the project to begin to explore possible ways of contacting women directly.

Two of the CAFAWs were interviewed as part of the review's assessment of the competence of *wasaidizi* in the different project areas. They were found to be very good in most of the criteria covered during the interview, and most of them felt that the most important knowledge they had acquired was on the correct dosages of medications and, in particular, the use of syringes for measuring de-wormers. There was a general feeling that modern medicines were superior to local *dawas* and some conditions (for example, wounds) were teated with wound powder from the CAFAW kits when local *dawas* were available. The pastoralists did not feel that they had learned anything about new diseases or disease recognition, and they were generally poor on improved husbandry practices. They had little knowledge of how legislation restricted their work.

A feedback seminar was held for all CAFAWs about a month after the first two training courses. Many of the issues raised were similar to those occurring in Meru – the long distances to be covered, little profit, wanting scheduled drugs, and difficulties of restocking drug supplies (in this case drugs were sometimes not available, while in Meru the complaint concerned the distances to be travelled to restock). During the first year of operation the CAFAWs' work rate seems to have declined, one reason being that profit margins are probably too small to encourage them to cover the enormous distances between households.

In addition, it has become apparent that there was a socio-cultural flaw in the project design for Pokot. Although all of the farmers met with as part of the review were pleased with the CAFAW training and the increased supply of drugs, information available indicated that there are not traditional animal health practitioners in the Pokot area. It appears that as a matter of cultural pride adult men feel that they should be able to diagnose and (to the extent treatments were available) treat their own animals. This is coupled with (and fed back into) the highly developed level of indigenous technical knowledge. Apparently many CAFAWs have already begun to train farmers in proper dosage rates, and there is strong pressure (from both farmers and CAFAWs) for future project activity to involve direct farmer training.

A second phase for the project has thus been designed in which CAFAWs will be encouraged to simply sell medicines to livestock owners, who will be trained directly in how to administer the correct dose of the correct drug for each of the common diseases. In addition, attempts will be made to improve the availability of drugs in the area by training selected individuals in their purchase, use and sale. The second phase will be implemented by KFFHC and EPAP alone, further assistance from KLP being limited to two surveys covering the existing knowledge and use of traditional and modern animal medicines in the area, and existing commodity marketing institutions.

Utooni Development Project (UDP), Machakos District

UDP is a small self-help group in Machakos which has a number of activities, such as water tank construction, income-generating projects and a private technical training institute. In mid-1988 it asked ITDG to help establish a livestock project, including the training of barefoot vets. The project covers three administrative locations in Kilome Division, and an area of approximately 180km^2 which is ecologically and ethnically quite homogeneous. There are about 5,300 households and 28,000 people according to the 1979 census (current numbers are, as in Meru, likely to be 25 to 50 per cent higher). Ninety per cent of the project area falls in one agro-ecological zone (zone 5, of medium potential, similar to the Meru site).

The area is mainly inhabited by Wakamba who have gradually migrated there from better-watered locations, bringing with them production technologies which many researchers feel are unsuited to their new abode. As in Meru, land registration is underway, but already

24

clan control of land has diminished; most land is under the control of extended families (*musyi*), comprised normally of a man, his wives and married sons (and occasionally daughters). Land is allocated to sons at marriage, so each *musyi* has several 'independent' households. As in much of Kenya, land is considered scarce; while farm sizes may appear large, the potential is low.

Historically the Wakamba were hunters and livestock keepers who evolved into agriculturalists when they migrated to high potential areas, and now in Machakos they might best be described as mixed farmers. Livestock play a critical role in the project area, providing both food and income and an important source of drought security. In good years the Wakamba invest in livestock which they sell in dry years for survival. The use of manure and animal traction are important components of the agricultural system.

Data, paralleling that presented for Meru on the Machakos project site, can be found in Tables 4 and 5, Appendix 2. As in Meru, farm size and animal ownership (with the exception of chickens) are clearly correlated with wealth. Thus the KLP project aimed at meeting the needs of poorer farmers by placing more emphasis on smallstock and chickens and less on grade cattle (as happened in Meru). However, grade cattle were not completely ignored as it was felt that if the élites did not support the project its sustainability would be lessened and, in addition, the project partners had expressed an interest in grade cattle from the outset of their association with ITDG.

Data collection

Compared to Meru much less time was available for the initial, qualitative research which ideally precedes formal questionnaire design, including a review of existing literature.[13] KLP depended on local key informants and visits from the ITDG social scientist to provide the information necessary for project design. A two-stage quantitative data collection procedure was adopted. The first formal survey was administered to 109 farmers in seven villages, using a wealth-rank stratified sample. The villages were chosen to represent the slightly different situations found in the area in terms of land size and livestock distribution, and village elders were asked to describe the differences between them. This information was used by project staff to select the villages for the first survey.

This survey included basic information on farm and household size, crops grown (and their use), livestock kept, household and permanent hired labour used, major sources of livelihood (including both kind and cash income) and marketing of livestock. The exercise was coupled with what have become more or less standard data collection instruments for KLP, namely progeny histories (to record the fate of livestock offspring born on the farm) and ethno-veterinary studies. Initial investigations did not record the felt needs of farmers and requests for help, which it was planned would be covered in an end-of-year final survey. However, from secondary sources it was known that animal health and fodder problems represented important constraints to livestock – and hence crop – production.

Much more attention was paid to traditional healers in Machakos than in Meru. Detailed interviews were carried out, and a workshop was organized, in part so that they could contribute to the design of the CAFAW training courses. Perhaps more important than the 'technical' information the healers provided were their perspectives on their own roles and the lack of interest of the young in, and hence the loss of, indigenous technical knowledge. It was also noted that poorer people tended to use healers rather than the established veterinary service, as the traditional treatments were cheaper. All this information had important implications for project design. The initial survey work in the seven villages of Machakos was followed by a year-long, multiple-visit survey (completed in November 1989) to eight households in each of two villages. Villages and individuals for these case studies were chosen on the basis of further discussions with project staff and community members and the preliminary results of the first survey. The content of the case studies included activity profiles (labour data on a 24-hour recall), general sources of income (and cash income for livestock),

26

livestock-related expenditure, herd/flock changes, disease and problem reports and intra-household decision-making about animals.

Training of wasaidizi
In the first year KLP trained project staff to undertake the detailed socio-economic survey and held a workshop to discuss the results with the communities involved. A small *duka ya dawa* was opened as part of the Utooni general store and stocked with animal health products. Fourteen local men and women were trained and equipped to work as *wasaidizi*. In the first six months following training they treated 4,024 cases, attending 1,146 farmers. Most of the treatments were for worms, followed by fleas, lice and ticks. The *wasaidizi* also sold drugs to farmers.

User perceptions and recommendations for future activity
As in Meru, relatively little information was initially obtained about the social organization and socio-economic status of the project communities in Machakos. Thus there are uncertainties as to possible biases in the dissemination of information on, and availability of, *wasaidizi*, particularly relating to the effect of membership of UDP. A suggestion that non-group members be charged a higher rate for CAFAW services was fortunately rejected, but Utooni has the reputation of serving the needs of richer farmers, for example its interest in cattle upgrading and artificial insemination. In addition it appears that survey work was and is being conducted only in Utooni central villages, and seven of the first sixteen CAFAWs trained come from UDP's central group with only one each from various 'satellite' groups. The Utooni CAFAWs are either group members or relatives of members; yet group members are only 132 of perhaps 3,000 households.

However, some of the information collected during the review suggests that the actual delivery of CAFAW services is fair, and further investigations will be required (perhaps as part of a follow-up survey) to determine whether the apparent biases have any practical effects. In

27

addition to providing this information, a further survey, perhaps of the original 109 farmers, would be a source of feedback and assist in assessing the dissemination of information about CAFAWs and evaluating their use in the community after training.

The review's interview with two Machakos *wasaidizi* found that, with just over a month's experience, they were not as competent as their counterparts in Meru and east Pokot. They were wanting on most criteria, but time and frequent follow-up by extension workers should remedy deficiencies in knowledge and technique. Inspite of the efforts made to involve traditional healers in training courses, their relationship with the CAFAWs is not clear. This problem should be addressed, as the support of the healers will be necessary for incorporating traditional knowledge into courses and getting traditional remedies re-accepted.

A two-year second phase for the project was planned. It includes training a further 45 *wasaidizi* in areas surrounding Utooni, further training of existing and new *wasaidizi* to cover new diseases and Newcastle disease vaccination, and strengthening liaison between *wasaidizi*, the community and local government staff so that the *wasaidizi* can continue to work with less support from UDP. In addition, specific constraints faced by poorer livestock owners in fodder production and general management will be identified and appropriate training courses developed.

Oxfam, Samburu District

Oxfam (UK) in 1989 asked ITDG to help set up a decentralized animal health project as part of their wider community development programme in Baragoi Division, Samburu District. KLP will help them to undertake a baseline survey and will provide some staff training. It will also help in training local people to set up small *dukas ya dawa* where they can sell *dawa* and give advice to livestock owners. At the same time, the project will hold field seminars for livestock owners on the recognition and treatment of common, simple diseases.

As the project is just underway it is not possible to provide detailed information on the site or project activities. However, initial plans have

28

been made for data collection activities. Oxfam has a number of staff posted in the Baragoi area, many of whom are local and hence can and have served as key informants. A literature review on the area and its peoples is reasonably complete and is being verified with project officials and elders. This will serve to provide the basic background and socio-political information which is essential for deciding if the unit should be wealth ranked, as well as the unit for community contact. Plans to elicit information on livelihood and means of production using similar techniques are in place.

A combination of informal and formal data collection techniques will be used, including KLP's 'standard repertoire' (ie. wealth ranking, progeny histories and ethno-veterinary information). The approach in Samburu reflects the benefits of the experiences of designing DAH programmes in three other areas. Staff have a clear notion of the minimum types of data required and ways of collecting them. Although the depth of data of each type collected will not be very great, so that future monitoring will not have a detailed baseline upon which to draw, the data should be ample for project design and some follow-up evaluation.

DISCUSSION AND CONCLUSIONS

When KLP started it was realized that animal health was a problem, that services were not reaching farmers and that some sort of DAH would be useful, but what exactly was needed and how to go about it were unknown; the project had no ready-made technical package to extend. By 1989 the programme had made some progress towards answering these questions, and had tested one form of DAH in several project sites in differing circumstances. The review shows that DAH complements the activities of the established veterinary service in Kenya and can enhance its overall effectiveness.

In terms of improving the provision of animal health services, the programme's approach seems to have worked well in the settled areas such as Meru and Machakos, but to have been less successful in pastoral situations such as Baringo. Reasons for this were identified in the review and, as described in the previous section, it seems that a different form of training – involving livestock owners directly – would be more appropriate in pastoral areas.

The technical content of the programme
The focus
Given the seriousness of disease problems among livestock in the country, the inadequate coverage of existing veterinary and animal health extension services and the absence of any concerted effort on the part of other development agencies to address the animal health problem, there is little doubt that KLP's decision to concentrate on animal health was both timely and prudent. Within the animal health programme the main emphasis has been in the control of helminth and tick-borne diseases. Again, the high incidence of these diseases in the country and the substantial economic losses attributed to them justify this emphasis. It is recommended that KLP keep abreast with current research on the use of anti-helminthics, and it may even be possible for the programme, with the help of project partners (such as EPAP), to carry out some research work in this area.

In the course of time, however, as expertise on DAH is developed by other organizations, KLP's direct involvement in this type of activity should decline. Now is the time to begin investigating areas for future work, and the programme should be thinking about other appropriate technical interventions which could improve livestock production for poorer farmers. From farmers reports it is clear that there are a number of other serious livestock problems, such as feed shortages and management of young stock. In addition, several of the current project partners have expressed an interest in more broadly-based livestock development programmes.

Data collection

Data collection activities are a crucial aspect of KLP's attempt to achieve a 'socially sensitive' technical approach. Various factors influenced the extent and depth of data collection which could be undertaken for each of the projects, including their sequencing, proposed technical content, and the nature and wishes of project partners. In addition, in terms of social organizational information, the programme was hampered by the lack of well-developed methods for rapid appraisal of rural social structures.[14]

KLP used several fairly standard formal techniques for collecting, analyzing and using data, and these techniques are evolving towards the simplest way to obtain and use the minimum data set (see pages 32-3). However, further refinement is necessary, particularly in areas such as the time, training and resources required, the balance between the collection of quantitative and qualitative data, and the role of secondary literature and key informants. Although project partners may serve as valuable key informants, it is essential to understand how their responses might be biased by their role in the project and the community.

To date, data collection activities have been reasonably successful in providing the information necessary for project design and monitoring. However, there are indications in some of the projects that biases might be occurring in community outreach, the training of *wasaidizi*, the delivery of services, and types of animals and diseases

31

Minimum data set

KLP's experiences to date in assessing the needs for and designing and implementing DAH have provided sufficient information to begin to define a minimum data set which would be required to establish DAH programmes elsewhere in eastern Africa.[15] The data set is described below in terms of the types of data required, presented in the order of their collection; the depth of detail of data collected would depend on the requirements of the users. Data can be collected from secondary sources and key informants, or by more formalized methods such as questionnaires and farmer interviews.

Socio-political information

The primary purposes of this information are to understand and choose the unit of analysis (household/production unit), to understand and choose the unit of community (for wealth ranking, organization of people's input, feedback, etc.), and to understand potential factions which might affect the equitable delivery of programmes.[16] The information should enable the project to describe the household, including divisions of production/ consumption; levels of socio-spatial community organization, e.g. compounds, neighbourhoods, village; the main types of cross-cutting ties, e.g. clans, age sets, religious affiliation (do these create factions in the community?); the groups functioning in the community; and the most important egocentric networks, e.g. in-laws, mother's kin, stock friends.

treated. Thus specific areas were identified in the review for further investigation. These included social organization and group composition, particularly regarding the role of women in animal health care, traditional healers and indigenous technical knowledge.

In future, as the focus of the programme changes, further information may be required on other areas of livestock production. In this respect, as with information on animal health, the types of questions

32

Information on livelihood

The primary purpose of this information is to provide a basic understanding of sources of livelihood for households, with particular emphasis on the role of agriculture. Information should be sought for different agro-ecological zones within a project area and for households of different wealth rank. The information should include the main sources of livelihood and cash income and the general agricultural production system. Important factors in the latter would be access to land (main tenure type, control), labour (e.g. mainly household, compound, hired), capital and markets/shops; crops grown and their primary functions (sale, consumption, fodder); and types of livestock kept and their most important functions. Information should also be obtained on divisions within households of responsibility and product, especially for livestock

Livestock focus

The purpose of this information is to describe the importance of animal health as a constraint to production, detailing the most important diseases and farmers' understanding of health-related issues. Information should be provided on the primary constraints to production perceived by farmers/outsiders; primary diseases (serious and simple); indigenous technical knowledge with regard to disease and treatments (by the average farmer and local 'experts'); existing indigenous 'vet' services, including type, frequency of use, and mode of access; and the structure of the government veterinary service, including the number and type of personnel and its use by farmers.

asked are important in obtaining a true picture of the situation. For example, progeny histories and case studies cover only sold livestock products; thus functions such as traction and manure, and longer-term drought security, might be missed. Again, just asking farmers about problems encountered during the past month might lead to them omitting ever-present difficulties, such as the availability of fodder, and provide a false understanding of their needs.

Training

Training is carried out at several levels and covers a wide range of subjects, ranging from technical training in animal health for government staff to simple feedback seminars for farmers, *wasaidizi* and project members. Much of the training has been directed at project partners' staff. Since the programme started over 26 seminars and courses have been held, covering: (a) training of trainers. Simple training of trainers courses were held for staff at Kamujini and Kositei so that they could contribute to the development of the training materials, and subsequently use and modify them and produce new ones as necessary;

(b) technical courses. These have included *wasaidizi* training courses at KFC, Kositei and Utooni, animal health workshops for technical assistants at Marimanti, a course on the treatment of common serious livestock diseases for extension workers and government staff at Kositei, and courses in chicken vaccination at Kamujini;

(c) business management. A series of courses in simple business management were held at Kamujini for staff involved in the medicine shop and for treasurers of some nearby women's groups;

(d) feedback seminars. Survey feedback seminars and post-training feedback seminars have been held at both Kamujini and Utooni;

Training and monitoring of wasaidizi

Training is a central component of the KLP (see box, above). For the review a small number of *wasaidizi* from each project area were inter-viewed to assess their technical competence. This technique has obvious limitations and is no substitute for long-term monitoring and follow-up of all trainees. It can, however, identify any gross misconceptions or misuse of drugs in the treatment of common diseases. The training seems to have been reasonably successful in transferring skills, but how well *wasaidizi* subsequently worked varied from project to project and the interviews showed marked differences in their own perceptions about what they had learned and what was useful. Factors

34

(e) traditional healers' workshop. A workshop to discuss various aspects of traditional animal medicines was held at Utooni for local traditional healers;

(f) decentralized animal healthcare in pastoral areas. A workshop on the provision of decentralized animal health care in pastoral areas was held at Kositei for staff from pastoral projects supported by Oxfam;

(g) general livestock. A one-week course, 'Developing a Livestock Development Programme', was held at Kamujini for staff from agricultural projects supported by World Neighbours.

The structure of the training courses is based on a combination of skill transfer and awareness-training techniques.[17] Thus the courses combine discussion, often initiated by exposure to practical situations or to pictures or role-plays, with carefully structured practical training sessions in which skills are broken down into their component parts, and participants have the opportunity to practise them in a controlled environment. Instruction plans, training materials (posters, etc.) and participant handouts have been prepared for most of the courses, and are modified and updated as the courses are repeated.

such as their previous level of knowledge and experience with livestock and capacity for independent learning obviously influenced *wasaidizi*'s technical ability, in addition to the duration and level of their experience as an *msaidizi* and the extent of follow up training.

Aspects of *wasaidizi* training which could be generally strengthened seem to be the use of alternative drugs, the legal restrictions on and the dangers of misuse of antibiotics, and the role of improved livestock management in the control of disease. In all project sites more thought should be given to the balance of resources devoted to training intermediaries – as opposed to specialist farmers – in terms of the trade-

35

off between the cost of training *wasaidizi* and their likely coverage. Direct farmer training in each area should include recognition of common diseases and, in the pastoral areas, additional advice on treatment.

For the purposes of monitoring the work of *wasaidizi* following training, the records currently being kept (see page 38) seem to be sufficient at the moment. The data on the summary sheets give a simple 'at-a-glance' picture of the amount of work done each month, both by the service as a whole and by individual *msaidizi*, enabling project staff to monitor their progress and detect any sudden changes in working patterns which may require investigation. The keeping of records also reinforces to *wasaidizi* their responsibility to their communities and clients, as well as serving as a safety net in case of disputes. More detailed analysis of the records will help in planning future training courses and enabling comparisons across project areas, and it may be that additional data will be considered desirable in the longer term.

KLP's relationships with project partners

Central to KLP's mode of operation have been its relationships with project partner organizations. It is particularly important that the real, rather than rhetorical, goals of potential project partners match those of ITDG, especially in terms of a poverty- and community-based focus.

In future KLP needs to pay more attention to the mandate, structure and mode of operation of potential project partners. In terms of the 'capacity building' of partner organizations, specific areas were identified in the review where further staff training was required, for example in the training of trainers and the skills necessary for analysing data and translating it into information which could be used to direct the future course of a project. Project partners will vary greatly in the speed with which they can become autonomous, and the quantity and type of assistance they need. Although not an original intention, KLP's experience has suggested that thought should be given to increasing the extent to which projects may be more or less operational (at least for a time). However, the degree of operationalization would need to be flexible and must itself be socially sensitive, depending on the level of organization of the community involved.

KLP has tried to maintain the 'middle ground' between a purely technical assistance organization and one concerned with local-level community development. However, experience has shown that a combined approach requires more time and resources than more narrowly-defined technical assistance. Not all projects should have the same mix of technical assistance and community development – different peoples (communities and project partners) will be at different stages of development and hence have different requirements. At each stage of operation it must be clear what the relative balance of effort should be between these two types of objectives, and the approach needs to be taken into account in budgeting and evaluation.

Sustainability

The concept of sustainability relates to many aspects of the programme, from technical knowledge to training and monitoring skills to drug supply and referral services, and depends on many different factors – social, cultural, economic and political. Thus the extent of, and time required to achieve, sustainability varies for different aspects of DAH within and between projects. What actually constitutes an 'outside' input also varies, depending on local circumstances.

The achievement of sustainability will probably be most success-ful where new practices, such as treatments and training skills, can be acquired and transferred through existing social and cultural mecha-nisms and become incorporated into the indigenous knowledge base. There is evidence that this already happened in some projects and may be actively encouraged in future, for example in Pokot where *wasaidizi* will begin to train farmers. The concept also applies to the supply of drugs and referral services – where these can be 'grafted onto' existing trading and communications networks. However, other skills in monitoring and follow-up are crucial to this process, at least at the start,

Monitoring

Detailed monitoring systems have been established at both Kamujini and Kositei. The wasaidizi and CAFAWs fill in a notebook every time they treat an animal or sell medicine, recording the date, the name of the farmer, the disease treated, the medicine used and the price charged. In Kositei, where a number of the CAFAWs were illiterate, a record book was designed using symbols for the various species of animal, diseases and types of medicine used which could be simply marked with a tick or cross, so that the only writing required was the date, the farmer's name and the amount charged.

At the shop, receipts are issued to all purchasers and a cash book is filled in with one line for each transaction. This information is used to calculate the quantities of drugs sold and purchased each month, which are recorded on a monthly monitoring sheet together with the drugs in stock and the cash in the cash box and bank account. Duplicates of wasaidizi's records are also kept at the shop, and data are transferred monthly to summary sheets for each msaidizi or CAFAW.

to ensure that the knowledge passed on is correct. Such skills, and mechanisms for their transfer, are rare and while they are necessary will probably remain an 'outside' input.

Cultural factors also relate to the role of intermediaries. Although in pastoral areas it has been realized that direct farmer training will be more appropriate in the longer term, in areas where the level of indigenous technical knowledge is lower, and farmers are more accustomed to relying on outside assistance for treating animals, intermediaries are likely to continue to have an important role. Various factors affect their sustainability, including the time it takes to treat and reprovision, the profit to be made and their social context. As profits are never likely to be large, *wasaidizi* will probably be most successful in communities where there is a strong service tradition, which in tribal culture implies treating the animals of close family and neighbours. This suggests that in such communities a large number of *wasaidizi* should be trained, each being expected to assist a small number of farmer acquaintances, which would mean that they also had time to maintain other sources of income.

In addition to monitoring and follow-up skills, more sophisticated training skills – particularly those relating to the training of trainers – will probably also take longer to become sustainable, at least at the community level. As well as the time necessary to acquire such skills, a crucial factor is the cost involved – of training the trainers and then maintaining them as they train others. It is questionable whether these skills are actually appropriate at the level of the individual community, and thus achieving sustainability may be a question of helping a community to understand where such expertise can be found and how it can be accessed.

The most important aspect of long-term sustainability is the ability to adapt to changing circumstances. In the context of DAH these might include, for example, the appearance of new diseases and changes in drug availability and government policy. Adaptability is probably the most difficult aspect to achieve, even where some level of sustainability has already been attained. For example, the transfer of skills through existing cultural mechanisms has been mentioned, but there is a critical difference between these skills and indigenous technical knowledge. The latter develops over generations, through 'trial and error', enabling farmers to actively respond to new circumstances, while DAH skills are at present mainly directive and uncontextualized. Thus in the long term more in-depth training will be required, encouraging farmers and *wasaidizi* to discuss their experiences and try new treatments.

Finally in relation to sustainability is the issue of government policy and relations. In its Sixth National Development Plan, the Kenya Government endorses DAH as a method of improving veterinary services and reducing the costs to the farmer and national economy of livestock disease. KLP should take advantage of this clear indication of government commitment to secure the support and involvement of

39

District Development Committees and the DVS in its existing programme, for example by involving local veterinary staff in projects and facilitating communications between them and *wasaidizi*. KLP's most significant contribution to the policy debate has been the development and implementation of a working model of DAH in different situations in Kenya, and linkages forged with and between other groups attempting similar programmes have helped in the sharing and consolidation of experience and have unified the pro-DAH lobby.

Outlook for the future

As outlined above and in the previous section, the review made recommendations on both KLP's general approach and specific areas of project activity, many of which will be implemented by the programme in its next phase. In the immediate future attention will be focused on consolidating KLP's experiences with DAH, expanding the areas covered and partners with whom it works, and preparing and testing guidelines for other organizations to use in the long term. Several new projects are planned in Kenya, for example in Turkana and on the coast.

As described in the introduction, the concept of 'barefoot vets' was originally taken by the Livestock Programme to Kenya from India. Realizing that it had accumulated a significantly greater body of experience, the programme was, by the end of 1990, considering if such an approach to the provision of animal healthcare services could usefully be applied elsewhere. Thus opportunities were at that stage being explored in other African countries and in areas of India. Investigations were also underway in Nepal, where it is already government policy to train animal health workers in rural areas.

A form of DAH, similar to that adopted by KLP, has begun evolving in some developed countries, supported by the veterinary establishment. In the UK vets are running training courses and supplying medicines for their clients to treat common animal diseases.

Thus it is hoped that the Kenya Livestock Programme has demonstrated an approach to animal healthcare which will have considerable potential for poor livestock owners in many communities throughout the world.

40

NOTES

1. Government of Kenya 1989, *6th Development Plan – 1989-93*.
2. Government of Kenya, Rift Valley Province, Dept. of Animal Production 1987, *Annual Report, 1987*.
3. Government of Kenya, op. cit.
4. Information in the remainder of this chapter is based on the *1987 Annual Report of the Department of Veterinary Services*, Rift Valley Province (RVP). RVP provides a good case study for estimating livestock disease incidence in Kenya as a whole because:
   - it is the largest province in Kenya, consisting of 13 districts
   - it exhibits the greatest agro-climatic diversity
   - it supports 38 per cent of the country's total cattle population and 47 per cent of the sheep and goat population.
5. Allonby, E. W. and Preston, M. 1979, *The influence of breed on the susceptibility of sheep to H. Contortus infections in Kenya*, African Small Ruminant Research and Development.
6. Dunn, 1978.
7. Wellcome Kenya Limited, 1983.
8. One tropical livestock unit (TLU) is 250kg liveweight, equivalent to one cow or 10 goats.
9. Full documentation is available in Young, J., *Livestock Production in Lower Meru*, ITDG (internal document), 1987.
10. Wealth ranking: Once the community to be wealth ranked is chosen, a list of the names of all household heads, including females, is obtained, usually from an elder of the community. Each name is written on a small card, and informants from the community are asked in turn, and in private, to organize the cards into piles according to their own concept of the 'wealth' of each household. Scores are then averaged arithmetically and each household assigned a score and position along the wealth spectrum. The spectrum is then divided into the top 30 per cent (wealth rank 1), the middle 40 per cent (wealth rank 2) and the bottom 30 per cent (wealth rank 3). A small number of households are selected from each wealth rank to be interviewed. For further details, see Grandin, B., *Wealth ranking in smallholder communities: a field manual, 1986*.
11. Given the limited resources available for data collection, the ITDG project benefited immensely from the availability of an anthropologist, M. Bollig, who was working in the Pokot area during project implementation. Throughout the first phase of the project he served as a key informant on issues ranging from disease names and livelihood strategies to social organization. Much of the qualitatative data presented in this section is based on discussions of the reviewers and project staff with M. Bollig and/or are taken from his research dissertation.
12. The overall figure for animals treated is somewhat inflated by the work of one CAFAW in Chepelion, a highland area where ticks are a serious problem. In the first five months of work he treated 450 animals for ticks, mainly through the hand

41

washing of goats with Delnav. In the five months after receiving the spray pump he treated 1,381 animals for ticks, apparently mainly by spraying. In June 1988, however, a dip was opened in Chepelion. Although monitoring records post-June were not available, it was reported that the CAFAW had stopped such large-scale spraying of animals.

13. Literature on Machakos is super-abundant due to the large-scale Machakos Integrated Development Programme.

14. ITDG's proposed manual on social science applied techniques should contribute to the programme's ability to close this information gap.

15. The minimum data set would not be sufficient, however, for projects aiming for a broader involvement in livestock development.

16. Particularly in pastoral areas, where access to resources is communal, it is imperative to determine the mechanisms through which they are obtained and controlled.

17. The former borrow extensively from the methods developed by the Agricultural Training Board (ATB), UK, and are designed to give participants the maximum opportunity to practise and share their own experiences so that they learn by 'doing' and 'discussing' rather than by being told. The latter are based on the DELTA (Diocesan Leadership Training) courses developed by the Catholic Development Education Service (CDES) as part of their adult literacy training in the late 1970s and early 1980s.

Appendix 1: The objectives of the Agriculture and Fisheries Sector and of the Kenya Livestock Programme

The Kenya Livestock Programme is a part of ITDG's Agriculture and Fisheries Sector, which focuses on primary food production for consumption or the generation of income. The sector's objectives are to:
(a) improve the food production capability, for direct and indirect consumption, of resource-poor rural households;
(b) enable these households to improve access to, and have control over, the resources they use in production;
(c) assist in the development of institutional mechanisms whereby improvements in the conditions of resource-poor households can be maintained and built upon;
(d) assist in the dissemination of the above food production strategies – through training, exchange visits (including consultancies), seminars and publications – to other groups of resource-poor households.

KLP's long-term objectives are to:
(a) increase the productivity of livestock through improved health care and management;
(b) improve the integration of livestock-keeping within mixed farming systems;
(c) help communities to develop the most appropriate offtake and marketing systems for their particular socio-economic and cultural environment;
(d) ensure that livestock production systems do not erode the environment;
(e) help communities to strengthen their organization and control over the resources required for, and benefits derived from, livestock keeping;
(f) improve the legal and policy environment for livestock production, especially for poorer producers.

In order to achieve these objectives, in the short and medium term, the programme planned to:
(a) identify a range of suitable project partners;
(b) provide appropriate inputs to improve their capacity to implement livestock development projects, including staff training, technical advice and institutional development;
(c) assist the project partners to implement the projects;
(d) monitor the results of the projects;
(e) disseminate the results of the projects to other project partners, and to other government and non-government organizations;
(f) become involved nationally and internationally in the legal and policy debates relating to livestock development.

Appendix 2:   Social, cultural and livestock data for the project sites

Table 1: General information for the Meru project sites

	Tigania	Tharaka
Rainfall (mm)	800-2,200	650-850
Main crops	Maize, beans, bananas, coffee tea	Sorghum/millet maize, pulses sunflower, cotton
Livestock	Local, grade cattle smallstock, hens	Local cattle only smallstock, hens
Cash income sources	Crop and livestock sales, business, wage labour, brewing	
Drought income	Livestock sales, business, wage labour	
Number of households	9,000	
Total livestock	Grade cattle 1,400 Local cattle 33,500 Goats/sheep 86,150 Chickens 126,200	

Source: ITDG (internal document), 1987 Young, J., *Livestock production in lower Meru.*

Table 2:   *Household level information for the Meru site by wealth rank*

Wealth rank	WR 1	WR 2	WR 3	Mean
Household size	9.3	7.6	7.1	8.0
Farm size (ha)	5.6	3.6	2.5	3.8
Cultivated (ha)	2.6	1.6	1.2	1.8

Number of animals owned
(and % households owning):

Grade cattle	2(26)	1(4)	0(0)	2(10)
Local cattle	11(84)	5(73)	4(33)	7(64)
Goats/Sheep	39(84)	15(75)	10(59)	22(73)
Chickens	0(98)	0(95)	0(90)	17(95)

Note: In Meru, wealth rank 1 and 3 represent the most wealthy 30% and the least wealthy 30% of the population, with 2 being the middle 40%.

Source: ITDG (internal document), 1987 Young, J., *Livestock production in lower Meru.*

Table 3:   *Rough estimates of mean household livestock holdings in the KFFHC project sites*

Area	Camels	Cows	Goats	Mean TLU owned by households among the Richest 25%	Poorest 25%
Kechii	2.5	57	114	142	24
Chesanja	1.5	22	65	82	6
Chepelion	0	37	120	91	3
Kakapul	0	30	70	63	7
Chemsik	3.5	25	37	49	13
Mean	1.5	34	81	85	11

Source: Adapted from Young, J., 1987.

No. of households in the project area   4,211
Source: 1979 census.

Livestock in the project area	Camels	2,060
	Cattle	41,160
	Goats/Sheep	60,000
	Donkeys	5,000

Source: Divisional veterinary officer, Nginyang.

46

Table 4: General information for the Machakos project site

Rainfall (mm)	700-950
Main crops	Maize, beans, sorghum, cassava, coffee, cotton
Livestock	Grade, local cattle, goats, sheep, chickens
Income sources	Crops, livestock sales, wages and pensions
Number of households	5,300

Total livestock		
	Grade cattle	1,320
	Local cattle	23,400
	Goats/Sheep	40,680
	Chickens	34,000

Source: Njeru, F., Survey.

Table 5: Information for the Machakos project site by wealth rank

Wealth rank	WR 1	WR 2	WR 3	WR 4	Mean
Household size	8.4	8.4	7.0	7.6	7.8
Farm size (ha)	12.3	6.5	5.6	5.5	7.5
Cultivated area (ha)	5.5	2.9	3.4	2.3	3.5
Number of animals owned (and % households owning):					
Grade cattle	2(27)	1(8)	0(0)	0(0)	1.3(7)
Local cattle	8.6(95)	3.3(96)	4.2(18)	2.3(18)	4.3(55)
Goats	7.3(87)	5.8(88)	4.6(78)	4.3(75)	5.6(87)
Sheep	4.4(72)	2.5(58)	2.6(22)	3.5(40)	3.4(49)
Chickens	8.2(85)	7.5(81)	8.2(70)	4.6(75)	7.3(82)

Source: Njeru, F., *Some features of smallholder livestock production in lowland areas of Machakos District.* ITDG Survey, 1990.

Appendix 3: Disease incidence and the provision of veterinary services in the project areas

Table 1: Reasons for death of cattle and smallstock in Tigania Division, Meru District, 1986 (as % of deaths)

Cattle		Smallstock	Goats	Sheep
East coast fever	22	Parasitism	5	0
Anaplasmosis	3	Lung disease	36	0
Trypanosomiasis	8	Diarrhoea	0	32
Skin disease	2	Other disease	16	16
Diarrhoea	5	Birth problem	3	16
Other diseases	1	Accident/mishap	11	4
Accident/mishap	17	Drought	2	4
Drought	13	Predators	27	28
Unknown	29			

Source: ITDG survey.

Table 2: The commonest diseases affecting livestock in Tigania Division

	Farmers groups	Traditional healers	Vet staff
Anaplasmosis	+++	+	+++
Trypanosomiasis	++	-	+
East coast fever	+	++	+
Worms	+++	+++	+++
Pneumonia	++	++	++
Conjunctivitis	++	+	+
Mange	++	-	-
Nyongo	++	-	-
Dystochia	+	++	-
Foot and mouth	+	-	+
Circling disease	+	-	-

Source: As reported by farmers' groups, traditional healers and vets.

Table 3: Provision of veterinary services in the project areas

Division	Area (km²)	Households	Cattle	Sheep/goats	Camels	Donkeys
				Livestock ('000s)		
Nginyang	4,441	4,211	41	60	2	5
Tigania	652	26,157	54	72	1	
Tharaka	1,496	9,463	50	136		

Division	Total TLU	Total vet staff	Ratio of vet staff to TLU
Nginyang	49	13	1:3,780
Tigania	57	13	1:4,350
Tharaka	59	8	1:7,330
Kilome		14	

Sources: Veterinary officers, Nginyang, Tigania and Kilome Divisions;
Farm Management Handbooks, Vols. II, B and C.

*Table 4:Cause of death of animals in Nginyang Division, Baringo
District (as % of deaths)*

Camels %		Cattle %		Goats %	
Cholera	57	East coast fever	32	Diarrhoea	10
Ticks	9	Trypanosomiasis	11	Worms	7
Trypanosomiasis	4	Diarrhoea	4	Pneumonia	7
Skin disease	4	Cheptigon (ECF)	2	Mange	5
		Pneumonia	2	Orf	5
		Anthrax	2	Enterotox.	3
		Worms	1	Mange	2
		Ticks	1	Tryps	2
		Foot and mouth	1	Cherembes	1
		Mastitis	1	Ticks	1
		Bloody scour	1		
Drought/Injury etc.	2	Drought/Injury etc.	39	Drought/Injury etc.	58

Source: As reported by owners, ITDG survey, 1987.